# Discovering the Holy Spirit

By Brian Rezendes

# DEDICATION

*I dedicate this book to my three children.*

*May you grow to experience*

*the Promise of the Father for yourselves.*

# TABLE OF CONTENTS

# INTRODUCTION

## Discovering the Holy Spirit

Have you ever been overlooked in church? Well then, you are in good company because so has the Holy Spirit. He is the most misunderstood, ignored, and sometimes even scorned Person of the Trinity in the church. Tragically, many Christians live their entire lives without ever experiencing the presence and power of the Spirit.

In my own Christian experience, I initially knew very little about the Holy Spirit; and nothing at all of being baptized with the Holy Spirit or that I could have fellowship with Him.

This book reflects what I have found in my journey through the Bible, the written Word of God, as I have sought to better understand and, more importantly, to experience the Holy Spirit in a greater way for myself.

The Word and the Spirit are not to be separated as is all too often the case in the life and experience of my Christians and churches. We must not settle for one without the other.

We must not emphasize one to the exclusion of the other. It is

with both the Word of God and the Spirit of God that

Christians can grow to maturity and more effectively impact the

world for Christ.

**Chapter 1**

# ANOTHER HELPER

*Nevertheless, I tell you the truth: it is to your advantage that I go away, for if I do not go away, the Helper will not come to you. But if I go, I will send him to you.*

John 16:7

Few among us would take it lightly to have Jesus Christ physically present in our midst. He fully revealed God the Father, regularly healed the sick, multiplied food, and instructed those that heard Him with His life-changing teaching. Yet it is Jesus Himself that made this startling statement. He said that it was to our "advantage" for Him to go away to Heaven in order for the Helper to come. Who was this "Helper" and how could it possibly be more advantageous to have Him than to have Jesus physically among us?

Earlier in John 14:16-17, Jesus identified this Helper as the Holy Spirit.

*And I will ask the Father, and he will give you **another*** ***Helper**, to be with you forever, even **the Spirit of truth**, whom the world cannot receive, because it neither sees him nor knows him. You know him, for he dwells with you and will be in you.*

John 14:16-17 emphasis mine

The Holy Spirit is "another Helper". "Another" in this passage is the Greek word *allos* meaning "another of the same kind", indicating the Spirit would be our Helper in every way Jesus was a Helper among His people. Jesus' departure to Heaven was therefore not to be a point of sorrow for the disciples as they now would have the Holy Spirit dwelling "in" them. Jesus was in some ways limited by His physical body during His earthly ministry, being only in one geographical location at a time and needing things like sleep and rest. The Holy Spirit, though the world cannot see Him, dwells with and in every one of us as Christians. We do not have to travel to Galilee or Jerusalem to talk with the Holy Spirit and receive from Him. This the Holy Spirit advantage. He is with you in your car on the way to work or in your living room when you come home.

## Heaven's Helper

The Helper, Greek *Parakletos*, means "one called alongside to help" and indicates the essential role the Holy Spirit has in our lives. As the *Parakletos*, He is our Comforter, Counselor, Intercessor, Advocate, Strengthener, and Standby.

### 1. Comforter

Wherever and whenever we are hurting, the Spirit of God is there to give us comfort. He heals the brokenhearted and brings peace to those that are in the midst of turmoil. We can invite Him to draw near to where we are hurting most and fully receive His comforting presence.

## 2. Counselor

As our counselor, the Holy Spirit teaches us. He is the One that opens our eyes to see and understand the Bible and ourselves. He is the One that lovingly corrects us and changes us to become like Christ in our words and actions. There is no problem we face where He does not have the answer.

## 3. Intercessor/Advocate

You have someone looking out for you! The Holy Spirit is continuously interceding on your behalf. In the court room of life, you have an Advocate Who has taken up your case. He is personally involved in defending and protecting you from the strategies of hell. Even when we do not know ourselves what to pray for, He does!

*Likewise the Spirit helps us in our weakness. For we do not know what to pray for as we ought, but the Spirit himself intercedes for us with groanings too deep for words.*

Romans 8:26

Holy Spirit directed prayers are in perfect accord with God's will (Rom. 8:27) and produce powerful results as He ensures "all things work together for good" (Rom. 8:28).

## 4. Strengthener

Where we are weak, He is strong in us. A life lived in dependence upon the Spirit of God is one that has discovered the inexhaustible source of strength to fight any battle and overcome any challenge life can bring.

## 5. Standby

As the *Parakletos*, He is right by our side even if no one

else is. He is there to sustain and guide us. What is overwhelming for you right now? Invite Him to help you and remember that He is with you forever as your Standby.

These descriptions of the *Parakletos* all illustrate His role as our Helper. Next, we will examine the Holy Spirit's witness and ministry to the world.

## Chapter 2

# THE WITNESS OF THE SPIRIT

*And when he comes, he will convict the world concerning sin*

*and righteousness and judgment: concerning sin, because they*

*do not believe in me; concerning righteousness, because I go to*

*the Father, and you will see me no longer; concerning*

*judgment, because the ruler of this world is judged.*

John 16:8-11

The three-fold convicting witness of the Spirit concerns sin, righteousness, and judgment. To convict is to expose, correct, or convince with proof. The world is clouded by spiritual and moral darkness. The Spirit of God comes to expose the nature of this darkness in order for men and women to come to salvation in Jesus Christ. Let's examine the three areas of conviction.

First, the Holy Spirit convicts the world of sin,

particularly the sin of unbelief. Sin is rebellion against God and ultimately brings death. It is sin that has separated man from God, thus resulting in eternal death. Jesus Christ paid the price for our sins, taking our place on the cross and receiving our just penalty for sin so that we may be reconciled to God and receive eternal life. The Holy Spirit is the One that awakens our hearts to the destructive nature of sin and convicts us of our need to turn from sin to Jesus Christ as our Lord and Savior. Sin holds the entire world under its deception, while the Spirit of Truth leads us away from that deception into freedom. Ultimately, it is not persuasive preaching or arguments but the ministry of the Holy Spirit touching the heart of an individual that convicts that person of their need for God.

The conscience of a person, having been seared by sin, is made sensitive to the Holy Spirit when that person comes to Christ. When Christians sin, we grieve the Spirit (Ephesians 4:30). Many recognize this grieving as the conviction of the Spirit by which we know that we have sinned and can repent. This exposes the lies and excuses we have believed, enabling us to experience greater freedom and become more like Christ.

As John the Apostle states:

*If we say we have no sin, we deceive ourselves, and the truth is not in us. If we confess our sins, he is faithful and just to forgive us our sins and to cleanse us from all unrighteousness. If we say we have not sinned, we make him a liar, and his word is not in us.* 1 John 1:8-10

Second, the Holy Spirit convicts the world of righteousness, because Jesus is no longer physically present in the world. It is the Spirit of God that testifies of Christ and His righteousness. This has the effect of both pointing the sinner to Christ and revealing the nature of His righteousness imputed to the believer's life. It is not enough to be convicted of sin and our need for God, but we must be led to the answer to that need. The Holy Spirit therefore points us to the answer found only in the righteousness of God that comes through faith in Jesus Christ (Rom. 3:22).

*For our sake he made him to be sin who knew no sin, so that*

*in him we might become the righteousness of God.*

2 Corinthians 5:21


Jesus did not just remove our debt of sin, but He gave us the gift of His righteousness in our salvation. Because Christians have been made the righteousness of God in Christ, we can walk in righteousness after the pattern of Jesus. The Holy Spirit teaches us how as we follow His leading and correction.

Third, the Spirit convicts the world of judgment. Connected with sin and righteousness throughout the Bible is the idea of judgment. A judge in human terms issues judgments from a court with the goal of restoring order to society, making wrong things right, vindicating the innocent, punishing an offender, and demanding restitution for those victimized. The Spirit of God reveals what God accomplished through Christ's atoning work and the resulting defeat of Satan, the ruler of this world. Through the death, resurrection, and ascension of Jesus, the ruler of the world was judged. Jesus declared this reality in the following:

> *Now is the judgment of this world; now will the ruler of this world be cast out.*

John 12:31

The Holy Spirit's witness provides evidence that Satan is defeated and Jesus is victorious. This three-fold testimony regarding sin, righteousness, and judgment reveals the condition of the world, the provision for the need of the world, and the complete victory of Jesus over the ruler of this world.

# Chapter 3

# BORN OF THE SPIRIT

*Jesus answered, "Truly, truly, I say to you, unless one is born*

*of water and the Spirit, he cannot enter the kingdom of God."*

John 3:5

After the Holy Spirit convicts people of sin and they respond to the Gospel through repentance and faith in Christ, they are then born of the Spirit. Jesus referred to this as being "born again" (John 3:3). The spirit of a man before being born again is dead because of sin (Eph. 2:1), but that man's spirit upon receiving Christ is made alive through the regenerating working of the Spirit inside of him. This is necessary for a person to both "enter the Kingdom of God" and also live as a Christian now on the earth.

*He saved us, not because of works done by us in righteousness, but according to his own mercy, by the washing of regeneration and renewal of the Holy Spirit,*

Titus 3:5

The Spirit of God takes up residence in the heart and life of the believer forever (John 14:16-17). The indwelling Spirit, referred to as the Spirit of Adoption (Rom. 8:16), from then on "bears witness with our spirit that we are children of God." (Rom. 8:16) We are adopted into God's family in fulfillment of Jesus' promise:

*I will not leave you as orphans; I will come to you.*

John 14:18

In the act of regeneration, the believer is also sealed with the Holy Spirit (Eph. 1:13). The Spirit becomes for us the guarantee, or down payment (2 Cor. 1:22), of our eternal inheritance in Christ. We have been sealed for the day of redemption (Eph. 4:30). This sealing assures us of our safe arrival into eternal life like a package that has been inspected, approved, sealed, and delivered.

Have you been born again through repentance from sin and faith in Jesus Christ? If not, turn now to Jesus and receive forgiveness of sins and the gift of eternal life.

> *Because, if you confess with your mouth that Jesus is Lord and believe in your heart that God raised him from the dead, you will be saved. For with the heart one believes and is justified, and with the mouth one confesses and is saved. For the Scripture says, "Everyone who believes in him will not be put to shame." For there is no distinction between Jew and Greek; for the same Lord is Lord of all, bestowing his riches on all who call on him. For "everyone who calls on the name of the Lord will be saved."*

Romans 10:9-13

## Chapter 4

# FELLOWSHIP WITH THE SPIRIT

*The grace of the Lord Jesus Christ and the love of God and*

*the fellowship of the Holy Spirit be with you all.*

2 Corinthians 13:14

A powerful result of the indwelling of the Spirit and the regeneration of the believer is the opportunity to have fellowship with the Spirit of God Himself. Fellowship (Greek *koinonia*) means to share or possess things in common between two people. We share all we are with the Spirit, and He shares all He is with us. Fellowship requires personal relationship and communication. God wants more than mere intellectual or doctrinal assent to His presence but personal encounter and experience with Him. He longs to share life with us more than we will ever know.

Fellowship with the Spirit is an essential element of the

Christian life. As we begin to acknowledge and respond to God in a personal way, we will learn to hear His voice. Too often Christians live without the knowledge that they can in fact hear God speak to them personally. In many theological circles, it is held almost as a cardinal doctrine that God is now silent toward His people because we now have the Bible. This however overlooks what Jesus said was to be characteristic of all Christians in all generations, "My sheep hear My voice, and I know them, and they follow Me" (John 10:27). Notice He did not say "My sheep read My Book". Relationship makes it necessary that I hear His voice and follow Him. God, of course, speaks to us primarily through His Written Word, and we must rightly discern what we subjectively "hear" from the Spirit by the objective test of the Bible. God will never speak to us in a way that contradicts or changes Scripture. Every day though, I am faced with decisions for which there is no specific verse or chapter in the Bible. To know what I should do, I must live in a relationship of dependence upon the leading of the Spirit and the voice of God.

Everyone possessing the Holy Spirit has the capability of hearing God. Jesus said

*"I still have many things to say to you, but you cannot bear them now. When the Spirit of truth comes, he will guide you into all the truth, for he will not speak on his own authority, but whatever he hears he will speak, and he will declare to you the things that are to come.*

John 16:12-13

Notice, the Holy Spirit will both guide AND speak us as His people. God is not silent. In fact, God is speaking all of the time. The real issue is whether or not we are listening to "what the Spirit says to the churches" (Rev. 2:7). When you adjust the frequency of your radio, you tune in to hear radio signals that were already passing by unrecognized. Like a radio, you can adjust your heart to pick up the signal of His voice. We adjust our hearts to hear God by prayer and studying the Bible. God speaks to us in many ways. Biblically, we know that He speaks through 1) a whisper [or still, small voice] to our hearts [1 Kings 19:12], 2) His peace [Col. 3:15], 3) prophecy [Acts 21:11], or 4) dreams and visions [Acts 2:17]. God frequently speaks so subtly to us that will miss His voice if we are not tuning our heart to listen. Why does He do it this way? God wants us to depend upon Him and walk closely with Him in intimate fellowship.

## The Spirit of Revelation

As Jesus revealed in John 16, the Spirit of God leads us into all truth (John 16:12). Christians need not be afraid of deception as long as they remain open to the leading and correction of both the Word and the Spirit. Because knowing and walking in truth results in freedom (John 8:32), we must allow Him to expose every lie we have believed about God and ourselves and then come into agreement with that truth.

He will also tell us things to come (John 16:13). No one truly knows the future except God and only He can prepare you for the days ahead. If I travel to a new city, I would much rather have a guide that has actually spent time in the city rather than another visitor who has no experience there. God has not only seen the future, but He is already there. He is the only capable guide into our future.

Do you have trouble remembering important things, especially God's Word? The Holy Spirit will help bring to your memory all things that Jesus has spoken (John 14:26). This promise was first applicable to Jesus' disciples who had the important task of recording the Lord's words in Scripture. However, it also points to the truth that the Holy Spirit will help us to remember everything God has taught us from His Word when we need it. When you pray for someone, the Holy Spirit can bring to your mind a passage of Scripture to speak directly to their situation.

The Holy Spirit testifies of and reveals Jesus to us (John 15:26). Some think that to even talk about the Holy Spirit or place any emphasis on His working in the church is to somehow take glory away from Jesus. I personally do not believe Jesus feels at all threatened by any attention paid to the

Third Person of the Trinity. Whatever the Spirit does glorifies the Son and reveals His Person and redemptive work.

One of the primary ways He reveals Jesus is through declaring to us those things that belong to the Lord (John 16:14-15), things would otherwise be beyond our natural comprehension.

*But, as it is written, "What no eye has seen, nor ear heard, nor the heart of man imagined, what God has prepared for those who love him"--***these things God has revealed to us through the Spirit.** *For the Spirit searches everything, even the depths of God. For who knows a person's thoughts except the spirit of that person, which is in him? So also* **no one comprehends the thoughts of God except the Spirit of God.** *Now we have received not the spirit of the world, but the Spirit who is from God,* **that we might understand the things freely given us by God.** *And we impart this in words not taught by human* *wisdom but taught by the Spirit, interpreting spiritual truths to those who are spiritual. The natural person does not accept the things of the Spirit of God, for they are folly to him, and he is not able to understand them because they are spiritually discerned.*

1 Corinthians 2:9-14 emphasis mine

Paul here teaches that a major work of the Spirit of God in our lives is to make known to us those "things freely given us by God." He reveals to us Who Jesus is and what we have as our inheritance in Christ. An inheritance is something that someone has paid for and another receives for free. God "has blessed us in Christ with every spiritual blessing in the heavenly places" (Eph. 1:3). "Every spiritual blessing" is our inheritance which Christ has fully paid for, and it is by the revelation of the Spirit that we discover and by faith freely receive this inheritance for ourselves. Fellowship with the Spirit is a great adventure by which He takes us step by step through the treasure house of God's Kingdom.

## Led by the Spirit

> *For all who are led by the Spirit of God are sons of God.*

Romans 8:14

Spiritual maturity is not measured by how long we have been a Christian, how many books we have read, or conferences we have attended. Spiritual maturity is measured by how well we follow the leading of His Spirit. The sons (Greek *huios*) that Romans 8 has in mind here are mature sons. *Huios* is contrasted with *tekna*, which refers primarily to a child by birth. When my first son was born, the hospital put a band on his wrist that identified him as "baby Rezendes". He was my child by birth and name (*tekna*). As he has grown, he has matured and begun more and more to resemble me as his father both in appearance and behavior. A Christian is a child of God (*tekna*) by spiritual rebirth (John 1:12). As a Christian matures through being led by the Spirit on a daily basis, that person begins to look and act like their Father in Heaven. They are becoming mature sons (*huios*).

I like to compare fellowship with God's Spirit to sailing. When you discern the direction and force of the wind of the Spirit (John 3:8), you put up your "sails" by listening to and following His Voice. When He is not moving, you should not move either. When He is moving, you dare not remain still. Paul the Apostle, formerly Saul of Tarsus, began and continued his ministry on this very principle.

*While they were worshiping the Lord and fasting, **the Holy Spirit said**, "Set apart for me Barnabas and Saul for the work to which I have called them."*
Acts 13:2 emphasis mine

and

*And they went through the region of Phrygia and Galatia, **having been forbidden by the Holy Spirit** to speak the word in Asia. And when they had come up to Mysia, they*

25

*attempted to go into Bithynia, but* **the Spirit of Jesus did not allow them.** *So, passing by Mysia, they went down to Troas. And a vision appeared to Paul in the night: a man of Macedonia was standing there, urging him and saying, "Come over to Macedonia and help us." And* **when Paul had seen the vision, immediately we sought to go on into Macedonia, concluding that God had called us to preach the gospel to them.**

Acts 16:6-10 emphasis mine

When God's Spirit spoke, Paul and his companions listened. The results changed the world.

We must become sensitive to His leading, voice, and presence. To resist Him or His working is to "quench the Spirit" (1 Thess. 5:19). Let every one of us cooperate with Him and follow wherever and whenever He leads. The great reward of this fellowship is ultimately God Himself (Gen. 15:1) and the fulfillment of His will through our lives.

# Chapter 5

# Baptism with the Spirit

## My Introduction to the Baptism with the Holy Spirit

For many, the Person and Work of the Holy Spirit is either something that is misunderstood, feared, or ignored altogether especially when it comes to the Baptism with the Spirit and speaking in tongues. When I began to serve God in college years later, I knew very little of the Holy Spirit except that He was the One Who inspired the authors of the Bible (2 Tim. 3:16, 2 Pet. 1:21). So, I began to pray and ask the Holy Spirit to help me understand the Bible for myself. My assumption was, that since He wrote the Book, He could help me understand Scripture as its Author. My study of the Word of God that once was dry and confusing suddenly became alive as the Holy Spirit Himself became my Teacher.

I soon began to hear from others that there was something more to the ministry of the Spirit. They called it the Baptism with the Spirit. To learn more about the subject, I ordered a DVD from a respected Bible teacher that I hoped would explain this subject. While waiting for the DVD to come in the mail, I came a across a book on the subject which explained that the Baptism with the Spirit was an experience subsequent to salvation that was accompanied by speaking in tongues. This experience itself was a gift to be received like salvation, through faith. I prayed for this experience, though nothing initially happened. Later that same day, I attended a church that invited people to come to their prayer room after the worship service where they would receive prayer for the Baptism with the Holy Spirit.

After a brief explanation from the Bible, a pastor prayed for those in the room and many that had just received Christ as their Savior at the end of the worship service began to also now speak in tongues. Like earlier that day, nothing happened to me at first. The pastor came over, placed his hand on me and prayed for me personally. A few moments after the pastor stepped away, I had what I can only describe as a personal encounter with the presence of God. Something like a weight came upon me and then I too began to speak in tongues, in a language I had no prior knowledge or experience with. That evening, Jesus became more real to me that at any other moment since my conversion. He was the One that had baptized me personally with the Holy Spirit. What the Bible described in the Book of Acts, I was now experiencing for myself.

A week or two went by, and the DVD I had ordered came in the mail. To my surprise, the entire teaching contradicted my experience. The teacher stated emphatically that the Baptism with the Spirit was not a separate or subsequent experience to salvation but was the same thing; and the gift of tongues had ceased with the day of the Apostles in the first century church. Needless to say, I was very surprised. How could what I genuinely experienced not be from God? How could Christians and Bible Teachers have such differences of opinion concerning this experience? From that point, I began to search out what the Bible did itself say concerning the subject.

## What is the baptism with the Holy Spirit?

When Jesus was about to ascend to Heaven, having spent days teaching His disciples concerning the Kingdom of God and commissioning them to go into all the world, He gives them these final instructions:

*And while staying with them he ordered them not to depart from Jerusalem, but to wait for the promise of the Father, which, he said, "you heard from me; for John baptized with water, but you will be baptized with the Holy Spirit not many days from now."* Acts 1:4-5

This was no mere suggestion for the disciples. They were clearly commanded by Christ to wait. Had not Jesus told them previously to *go* into all the world? Of course, but there was evidently something the church needed before it could fulfill its assignment in the world. They needed the Promise of the Father. As John the Baptist had baptized with water, the disciples were to be baptized with the Holy Spirit. The word

used here for "baptized" is from the Greek root *bapto* meaning

"to dip". This word carries the idea of someone being

immersed in water (as with John's Baptism) and likewise

immersed in the Holy Spirit. The disciples were to be immersed

with the Spirit of God in Jerusalem in just a matter of days.

This experience occurred on the day of Pentecost as recorded

in Acts 2.

> *When the day of Pentecost arrived, they were all together in*
>
> *one place. And suddenly there came from heaven a sound like*
>
> *a mighty rushing wind, and it filled the entire house where they*
>
> *were sitting. And divided tongues as of fire appeared to them*
>
> *and rested on each one of them. And they were all filled with*
>
> *the Holy Spirit and began to speak in other tongues as the*
>
> *Spirit gave them utterance.*
>
> Acts 2:1-4

While Jesus predicted that the disciples would be

baptized with the Holy Spirit, we find in Acts 2 that they were "filled with the Holy Spirit". This shows that the terms "baptized" and "filled" are closely connected if not synonymous. To be "baptized with" is to likewise be "filled with" the Spirit of God. What did this experience result in? The disciples "began to speak with other tongues, as the Spirit gave them utterance". The result was that the disciples spoke, not with languages they had learned naturally but with other tongues as the Spirit of God gave them the words.

The outpouring of the Spirit on Pentecost spilled out into the streets of Jerusalem where a crowd of people heard these Christians speaking in their own languages. Peter then began to preach with boldness to the crowd, explaining this event and proclaiming Christ Jesus. He tells them the following:

> And Peter said to them, "Repent and be baptized every one of you in the name of Jesus Christ for the forgiveness of your sins, and you will receive the gift of the Holy Spirit. For the promise is for you and for your children and for all who are

*far off, everyone whom the Lord our God calls to himself."*

Acts 2:38-39

Three elements to the experience of the Christian are expressed here. First, the people must repent, that is to turn from sin and place their faith in Jesus Christ. This is for salvation. Secondly, the people are instructed to be baptized in water, proclaiming publicly their faith in Jesus Christ. Thirdly, they are to receive the gift of the Holy Spirit. This three-fold message is echoed again in John's first epistle:

*For there are three that testify: the Spirit and the water and the blood; and these three agree.* 1 John 5:8 emphasis mine

It is the Blood (speaking of salvation), the water (speaking of the baptism with water), and the Spirit (speaking of the baptism with the Spirit) that all bear witness on the earth to Christ and the Gospel. Normal Christianity should include

all three: salvation, water baptism, and Spirit baptism. This was
foreshadowed in the Tabernacle of Moses. In the outer court of
the Tabernacle, there was a bronze altar where the sacrifice was
made (foreshadowing the sacrifice of Jesus for salvation) and a
bronze laver where priests were required to wash before entry
to the Holy Place (foreshadowing the baptism in water of
believers). The priests, before entering the interior of the
Tabernacle, were anointed with oil (foreshadowing Spirit
Baptism of believers).

Jesus Himself modeled this at His Baptism in the River
Jordan. Because He was without sin, He did not need
regeneration or salvation like we discussed in Chapter 3.
However, He was baptized in water, something every Christian
is to follow His example in. Then, after His baptism in water,
the Holy Spirit came upon Him. This is His baptism with the
Spirit. Luke 4:1 describes this as Jesus Christ "being filled with
the Holy Spirit". It is interesting to note that all of the miracles
of Christ followed this event. He did this to demonstrate and
model the normal Christian life: salvation, water baptism, and

Spirit baptism.

The three experiences are "for all who are far off, everyone whom the Lord our God calls to himself ". This means, we who are afar off can have the same salvation, the same baptism with water, and of course, the same fullness of the Holy Spirit that the Apostles and the first century church experienced. The church of the 21st century has as much a claim to the gift of the Holy Spirit as the early church. We have not been given nor should we expect anything less. The Book of Acts sets forth for us not only the history of the Church but the model for the church of every generation to follow. It is the same salvation, same Holy Spirit, and same promise to all (including you and me!).

## One Spirit, Two Distinct Experiences

The question remains, is the Baptism of the Spirit the same experience as that of the reception of the Spirit in salvation? To begin to answer this, we must look at the first account of the disciples receiving the Spirit of God, which contrary to popular belief was not on the day of Pentecost. In John 20, the Resurrected Christ appeared to them and showed the disciples "His hands and His side". Then He says and does the following:

> *Jesus said to them again, "Peace be with you. As the Father has sent me, even so I am sending you." And when he had said this, he breathed on them and said to them, "Receive the Holy Spirit."*
>
> John 20:21-22

This describes their regeneration or salvation experience. The disciples, who were up until now not yet "born again", at this time believed in the Resurrection of Jesus. He breathed upon them and stated that they were to receive the Holy Spirit in that moment. This event takes place many days, possibly even weeks, before Pentecost and their baptism with the Spirit.

The disciples, like all of fallen humanity, were spiritually dead before they believed. God, in the beginning, created man and breathed into him (Gen. 2:7) the breath (Hebrew *ruach* "breath, wind, spirit") of life. This living being, Adam, later became spiritually dead through sin. Jesus, having accomplished the work of redemption, breathes into His disciples just as God did in Genesis, only now it is regeneration through receiving the Spirit of God that is in view. The disciples are, in John 20, born again and receive the Spirit. However, there still remained for them to be baptized with the Spirit on the day of Pentecost. One experience was for regeneration and salvation, the other for empowerment (Acts 1:8).

The Book of Acts gives us further examples of the distinction between the regeneration by the Spirit and the Baptism with the Spirit as separate experiences.

First, in Acts 8, Philip the Evangelist journeys to the city of Samaria and proclaims Christ to them. His message is well received as it is not in word only but in the demonstration of the Holy Spirit and power (1 Cor. 2:4). In other words, the message was not just spoken but demonstrated through miracles that could be experienced. People were healed physically and delivered from evil spirits.

> *Philip went down to the city of Samaria and proclaimed to them the Christ. And the crowds with one accord paid attention to what was being said by Philip when they heard him and saw the signs that he did. For unclean spirits, crying out with a loud voice, came out of many who had them, and many who were paralyzed or lame were healed. So there was much joy in that city.*
>
> Acts 8:5-8

News traveled to the Apostles at Jerusalem about what was taking place. Their response is important to understanding the distinction between salvation and the Baptism with the Spirit:

> *Now when the apostles at Jerusalem heard that <u>Samaria had received the word of God</u>, they sent to them Peter and John,*

*who came down and prayed for them that they might receive*

*the Holy Spirit, for he had not yet fallen on any of them, but*

*they had only been baptized in the name of the Lord Jesus.*

*Then they laid their hands on them and they received the Holy*

*Spirit.*

Acts 8:14-17 emphasis mine


It is evident that the Samaritans had 1) received the
Word of God and been 2) baptized [in water] in the name of
Jesus. They have the first two aspects of what Peter proclaimed
at Pentecost: salvation and water baptism. It is evident that they
are Christians, are saved, and have everything that accompanies
such a salvation including regeneration by the indwelling Holy
Spirit. Yet John and Peter come to the Samaritans because
something was still needed, specifically the Baptism with the
Spirit. Please note that the text states that the Spirit of God
"had not yet fallen on any of them". It does not say that the
Holy Spirit was not "in" them. That is an important distinction.

Some Pentecostal groups misunderstand this passage to

teach that unless a Christian is baptized with the Spirit, they do not have the Spirit of God in them at all. This mistake comes from a misreading passages such as this and from combining the two experiences, salvation and the baptism with the Spirit. We must "rightly divide the Word" (2 Tim. 2:15 KJV). Scripture elsewhere is clear that in salvation, the Christian is regenerated by the Spirit and becomes indwelt by the Spirit of God.

All Christians that have received salvation have the Spirit of God; but many, like the Samaritans, have not yet been baptized with the Spirit. For this, Peter and John lay hands on them in order for the Samaritans to receive the Spirit. Again, that is not to say they did not have Spirit of God at all previously; but they now were filled with and immersed in the Holy Spirit. He was to be upon them as He had fallen upon the disciples at Pentecost. It is clear from this passage that the salvation of the Samaritans and their being Baptized with the Spirit were two separate and distinct experiences.

While the result of the Baptism with the Spirit is not stated as it was on the day of Pentecost, namely speaking in other tongues, there was some definite evidence of the experience as there was on Pentecost.

> *Now* **when Simon saw that the Spirit was given**
>
> *through the laying on of the apostles' hands, he offered them*
>
> *money,*
>
> Acts 8:18 emphasis mine

Simon saw something experiential happening among the Samaritans that let him clearly know the Holy Spirit was given through the laying on of hands. It was not something the Samaritans had by faith or in doctrine only but something experienced and visibly witnessed by those present. From comparing this story with other examples in Scripture, we can assume that this evidence that Simon saw was likely that they spoke with other tongues and/or prophesied.

Next, in Act 19, Paul comes to Ephesus and encounters "disciples" who "believed". Let's examine the story:

*And it happened that while Apollos was at Corinth, Paul passed through the inland country and came to Ephesus. There he found some disciples. And he said to them,* **"Did you receive the Holy Spirit when you believed?"** *And they said, "No, we have not even heard that there is a Holy Spirit." And he said, "Into what then were you baptized?" They said, "Into John's baptism." And Paul said, "John baptized with the baptism of repentance, telling the people to believe in the one who was to come after him, that is, Jesus." On hearing this, they were baptized in the name of the Lord Jesus. And* **when Paul had laid his hands on them, the Holy Spirit came on them, and they began speaking in tongues and prophesying.** *There were about twelve men in all.*

Acts 19:1-7 emphasis mine

It seems an odd question for Paul to ask the disciples whether or not they had received the Holy Spirit when they believed if, as Paul would evidently know, all believers are indwelt by the Spirit of God at conversion by necessity. However, it is apparent that Paul is pointing to a subsequent experience with the Spirit of God. The Baptism with the Spirit certainly can accompany the time when a person "believes" but can happen, as in my own case, sometime later.

The response of these disciples reveals that they have an incomplete experience, not only with Spirit Baptism but possibly with salvation and water baptism, as they have only experienced water baptism under John the Baptist. Whether or not they had previously believed in Jesus Christ is possible (John proclaimed Jesus as the Lamb that takes away the sins of the world); but it is clear that they were not baptized in His Name, which is why Paul does this for them. After baptizing them in water in the name of the Lord Jesus, Paul then lays hands on them, as Peter and John did the Samaritans, and "the Holy Spirit came on them". Notice again, that the Spirit did not come "in" them, something which occurs the moment someone believes. They are baptized with the Spirit following their being baptized with water. This is evidently a subsequent experience. Like Pentecost and the Samaritan outpourings, there was an experience that accompanied Spirit Baptism. Here, that experience is speaking with tongues and prophecy.

Last of all, we will look at Acts 10, which occurred after the Samaritan outpouring but before the example above in Ephesus. Peter is sharing the Gospel of Jesus Christ with what is to be the first Gentile converts, the household of Cornelius. While Peter was speaking, the Holy Spirit is poured out upon the listeners. This story is unusual because the Gentiles here received the Spirit Baptism before being baptized with water. They, like the Ephesian and Pentecost disciples, spoke in tongues when the Spirit of God fell upon them. This case included a slightly different order but shared the same results as other examples of Spirit Baptism.

*While Peter was still saying these things, the Holy Spirit fell on all who heard the word. And the believers from among the circumcised who had come with Peter were amazed, because the gift of the Holy Spirit was poured out even on the*

*Gentiles. <u>For they were hearing them speaking in tongues</u> and*

*extolling God. Then Peter declared, "Can anyone withhold*

*water for baptizing these people, who have received the Holy*

*Spirit just as we have?" And he commanded them to be*

*baptized in the name of Jesus Christ. Then they asked him to*

*remain for some days.*

Acts 10:44-48 emphasis mine

From the passages we have examined so far, we can conclude
the following:

    ·The Christian message includes a call to salvation,

    water baptism, and Spirit baptism

    ·The Baptism with the Holy Spirit is an experience

    distinct from salvation, though it can coincide with

    the experience of salvation and can precede water

    baptism

Brian Rezendes

•Speaking in other tongues accompanies and gives evidence to the reception of the Baptism with the Spirit (prophesying can also accompany this experience)

•The Baptism with the Spirit is given through the laying on of hands, though this is not the only method (as in Acts 10:44)

•The promise of the Baptism with the Spirit is for all believers of any generation

# Chapter 6

# Baptism with the Spirit (cont.)

## Speaking in other Tongues

> *And these signs will accompany those who believe: in my name*
>
> *they will cast out demons; they will speak in new tongues;*
>
> Mark 16:17

If the Baptism with the Holy Spirit is available for all

Christians, then the accompanying activity of speaking with

other tongues is as well. There are two major objections

commonly raised to this however. The first objection is that the

operation of tongues ceased with the early church following the

death of the Twelve Apostles and the completion of the New

Testament, according to an particular interpretation of 1

Corinthians 13. The second objection is that not all Christians

can speak in tongues as 1 Corinthians 12:30 seems to teach. To

properly answer these objections, we need to examine both of these passages.

## Objection #1-Tongues have ceased

*Love never ends. As for prophecies, they will pass away; as for tongues, they will cease; as for knowledge, it will pass away. For we know in part and we prophesy in part, but when the perfect comes, the partial will pass away. When I was a child, I spoke like a child, I thought like a child, I reasoned like a child. When I became a man, I gave up childish ways. For now we see in a mirror dimly, but then face to face. Now I know in part; then I shall know fully, even as I have been fully known.*

1 Corinthians 13:8-12

Some consider speaking in tongues to be no longer available or necessary today since tongues was intended by God to cease according to the passage above. I agree that this passage clearly teaches that both tongues and prophecy will one day cease. The issue is not if tongues and prophecy will cease but <u>when</u> they will cease. Also, they are not the only things which cease but knowledge as well. It is evident that the passage, written by the Apostle Paul to the Corinthians, makes not one reference whatsoever to the end of the early church, the death of the Apostles, or the completion of Scripture. These three (tongues, prophecy, knowledge) shall continue until "that which is perfect has come". Therefore, identifying the "perfect" is critical to understanding when these cease.

These three presently exist "in part", that is to say they are partial and limited. However, when the "perfect" comes, what is in part will be done away with or cease. Why? Because then, when the "perfect has come" we shall know, not in part, but fully. For then we shall see "face to face". We shall know just as we are known, fully and not partially. This is speaking of our future in eternity (the "perfect"), when we are face to face with God. We shall then know God as fully as we are known by God and not dimly as at present. There will be no need for tongues and prophecy in Heaven; however, they are necessary and available to us now in the present age of the church until the perfect finally comes.

## Objection #2-Not all speak in tongues

> *Do all possess gifts of healing? Do all speak with tongues?*
>
> *Do all interpret?*
>
> 1 Corinthians 12:30

The second objection addresses whether speaking in tongues is for <u>all</u> Christians. From the above passage, it seems clearly implied that not all speak in tongues. To answer this, we must understand the scriptural context. In 1 Corinthians 12 and 14, Paul the Apostle frequently discusses tongues and prophecy in their corporate expression in the church. 1 Corinthians 12 particularly describes how different gifts of the Spirit are distributed among the body of Christ, the Church. Paul's focus is not on laying out a detailed description of speaking in tongues but to instead focus upon how spiritual gifts were to be exercised properly in corporate gatherings of the church.

Paul throughout these passages refers to two different

aspects of speaking in other tongues, one as a gift for public and corporate expression in the church body, and the other for personal and private use in prayer and worship to God. It is in the first sense that not all possess the gift of tongues, as it is used in corporate expression; but it is in the second sense, for private practice, that tongues is available to all believers baptized with the Spirit. The corporate gift of tongues can and must be interpreted, according to Paul, for it to be understood by the hearers. The gift of tongues, when it is interpreted, edifies the entire church. Unlike prophecy and the gift of tongues, a personal prayer in tongues is not a message for the church but for prayer to God.

> *For one who speaks in a tongue speaks not to men but to God; for no one understands him, but he utters mysteries in the Spirit.*
>
> 1 Corinthians 14:2

Paul clearly practiced speaking in tongues himself.

*I thank God that I speak in tongues more than all of you.*

1 Corinthians 14:18

The promise of the Baptism with the Spirit is for all believers. Jesus stated that speaking in tongues would be an activity of those who believe (Mark 16:17). If a Christian does not speak into tongues, this in no way makes them less of a Christian. However, we should continue to pursue all that God has made available to us.

**Benefits of the Baptism with the Spirit**

*But you will receive power when the Holy Spirit has come upon you, and you will be my witnesses in Jerusalem and in all Judea and Samaria, and to the end of the earth."*

Acts 1:8

Receiving power from God is the primary benefit of the Baptism with the Spirit. Jesus poured out His Spirit upon the church so it could do the "greater works" (John 14:12) that He has called us to. The Christian life and ministry without the power of the Spirit is like a car with no engine. You can push the car with great difficulty, but when you add the engine, there is power that moves the car in ways you never could without it. The mission of the church needs the power of God received through the Baptism of the Spirit to see the Great Commission accomplished.

The power of the Spirit also gives us boldness, as it did the early church.

*And when they had prayed, the place in which they were gathered together was shaken, and they were all filled with the Holy Spirit and continued to speak the word of God with boldness.*

Acts 4:31

Connected to the Baptism with the Spirit is spiritual fire. Jesus baptizes us in both the Spirit and fire (Luke 3:16).

Every aspect of our walk with God is to be ignited with passion. This happens when a believer is Baptized with the Spirit.

**Benefits of Speaking in Tongues**

Accompanying the Baptism with the Spirit is the enablement to speak in other tongues. The following are a few of the Scriptural benefits of speaking in other tongues:

**1. Praying in tongues, synonymous with praying in the Spirit, grows our faith and builds up our spiritual lives**

> *But ye, beloved, building up yourselves on your most holy faith, praying in the Holy Ghost,*
>
> Jude 1:20

> *The one who speaks in a tongue builds up himself, but the one who prophesies builds up the church.*
>
> 1 Corinthians 14:4

## 2. Praying in tongues brings revelation or illumination to your spirit from God

> *But the anointing that you received from him abides in you, and you have no need that anyone should teach you. But as his anointing teaches you about everything, and is true, and is no lie--just as it has taught you, abide in him.*
>
> 1 John 2:27

## 3. Praying in tongues ignites and empowers our prayer life

> *Likewise the Spirit also helpeth our infirmities: for we know not what we should pray for as we ought: but the Spirit itself maketh intercession for us with groanings which cannot be uttered. And he that searcheth the hearts knoweth what is the mind of the Spirit, because he maketh intercession for the saints according to the will of God. And we know that all things work together for good to them that love God, to them who are the called according to his purpose.*
>
> Romans 8:26-28 KJV

When you are praying in tongues, the Holy Spirit is enabling your spirit to pray according to the mind and will of God. This is not limited by your own understanding.

*For if I pray in a tongue, my spirit prays but my mind is unfruitful.*

1 Corinthians 14:14

## One baptism, many fillings

While the Bible indicates that believers are to be baptized with the Holy Spirit, an experience that occurs only once in a person's life, there are evidently many times that a believer may be subsequently and repeatedly filled with the Spirit.

*And do not get drunk with wine, for that is debauchery, but be filled with the Spirit,*

Ephesians 5:18

In this passage above, the tense of the Greek word *plērousthe* translated "be filled" indicates that the believer is to be continuously being filled with the Spirit. This is an ongoing infilling rather than a single event. The context of the passage indicates that praise and singing to the Lord is a means by which we are continuously filled (Eph. 5:19).

Believers, including the Apostle Peter, had already experienced the Baptism with the Spirit on the day of Pentecost; yet after experiencing persecution, they prayed to God and were again "all filled with the Holy Spirit".

> *And when they had prayed, the place in which they were gathered together was shaken, and they were all filled with the Holy Spirit and continued to speak the word of God with boldness.*
>
> Acts 4:31

## Receiving the Baptism in the Holy Spirit

Now that we have studied the promise of the Baptism

with the Holy Spirit and examined its Scriptural examples and benefits, we shall finally turn to how we receive this wonderful gift for ourselves. To be baptized with the Holy Spirit you must first be a Christian, having repented and believed in Jesus Christ (Acts 2:38-39).

## 1. This Gift is received by faith

> *O foolish Galatians! Who has bewitched you? It was before your eyes that Jesus Christ was publicly portrayed as crucified. Let me ask you only this:* **Did you receive the Spirit by works of the law or by hearing with faith?** *Are you so foolish? Having begun by the Spirit, are you now being perfected by the flesh?*
>
> Galatians 3:1-3 emphasis mine

You must believe ("hearing with faith") that the Baptism with the Spirit is for you personally. You cannot earn the gifts of God by "works", but Jesus has freely provided you with this amazing gift by His grace.

## 2. Ask Jesus to baptize you with the Spirit and by faith receive this gift for yourself

> *And I tell you, ask, and it will be given to you; seek, and you will find; knock, and it will be opened to you. For everyone who asks receives, and the one who seeks finds, and to the one who knocks it will be opened. What father among you, if his son asks for a fish, will instead of a fish give him a serpent; or if he asks for an egg, will give him a scorpion? If you then, who are evil, know how to give good gifts to your children,* **how much more will the heavenly Father give the Holy Spirit to those who ask him!"**

Luke 11:9-13 emphasis added

## 3. You must speak out loud what the Holy Spirit gives you

> *And they were all filled with the Holy Spirit and began to speak in other tongues as the Spirit gave them utterance.*

Acts 2:4

The Holy Spirit does not force Himself. You must yield

yourself to Him and speak out of your own mouth what comes

to you.

# Chapter 7

# The Fruit of Spirit

*And the angel answered her, "The Holy Spirit will come*

*upon you, and the power of the Most High will overshadow*

*you; therefore the child to be born will be called holy--the Son*

*of God.*

Luke 1:35

The miracle of the Incarnation of Christ, in which the

Word was made Flesh (John 1:14), was accomplished as the

Spirit of God came upon Mary and His power overshadowed

her. Jesus was thus conceived by the Holy Spirit (Matt. 1:20).

While this is a unique event, it illustrates a powerful truth in the

relationship between Christians and the Spirit. It is the Spirit of

God that reproduces the character and nature of Christ in us.

The Written Word of God "becomes flesh" in us as we

through His power walk out Christ-likeness in our words,

61

nd actions.

In Galatians 5, Christians are instructed to "walk in the Spirit". This is a decision to follow God's Word and obey the leading of the Spirit. Overcoming sin is not accomplished by simply having a list of "thou shalt not's". God's Word tells us that by walking in the Spirit, a positive and preemptive action, we will "not fulfill the lust of the flesh" (Gal. 5:16). To walk in the Spirit enables the Christian to successfully resist and overcome temptation.

God's Spirit dwells within us and reproduces the life and nature of Christ through the nine characteristics or fruit of the Spirit.

*But the fruit of the Spirit is love, joy, peace, patience, kindness, goodness, faithfulness, gentleness, self-control; against such things there is no law.*

Galatians 5:22-23

Through abiding in fellowship with the Spirit, our lives

will produce these nine fruit. Each fruit is a characteristic of the nature of Christ that God wants to reveal in and through us to the world. Fruit contains seed, and every seed reproduces the nature of the plant it came from. When people in the world around us experience the fruit of the Spirit, such as love, displayed in our lives, then the seed of that fruit can potentially reproduce the nature of Christ in them if they receive it. People can become nourished, enriched, and forever changed by what God's Spirit brings through our lives.

# Chapter 8

# The Gifts of the Spirit

Just as the Holy Spirit enables us to display the character and nature of Christ through the fruit He produces in our lives, He also equips us with the power of Christ through spiritual gifts. We looked briefly in chapter six at the continuation of tongues in the church today. Now we will look deeper at the Gifts of the Holy Spirit and how we receive those ourselves.

Paul the Apostle, in 1 Corinthians 12, begins a discussion of spiritual gifts and their proper function in the life of the church with the following admonition:

> *Now concerning spiritual gifts, brethren, I would not have you ignorant.*

1 Corinthians 12:1 KJV

Discovering the Holy Spirit

The way we become ignorant of anything is by either
ignoring or misunderstanding it. The Corinthian church was
particularly guilty of the latter. They had ample experience with
spiritual gifts but had little proper order in how those gifts
functioned. Also, while they had powerful operations of the
gifts of the Spirit, there were a number of character issues that
had run unchecked among the Corinthians. They had gifts but
lacked fruit.

The opposite error is equally prevalent among those
that choose to ignore the gifts of the Spirit altogether. They
may place value on the fruit of the Spirit and Christian
character but either neglect or outright reject the present
operation of spiritual gifts such as prophecy and tongues. Paul,
warning us not to be ignorant, removed both of these options
and gave us only one appropriate choice, to embrace both the
gifts and the fruit of the Spirit. We must have both character
and power to fully demonstrate God's Kingdom in the world
and bear testimony to the Gospel. As Paul previously wrote to
the Corinthians, we must "...come behind in no gift" (1 Cor.

1:7 KJV).

A common error today is to reduce the spiritual gifts to some kind of natural talent or ability. However, 1 Corinthians lists at least nine spiritual gifts that are "manifestations" of the Spirit (1 Cor. 12:7) rather than products of human nature. The gifts are spiritual and supernatural because they are the workings of God in and through His people. To reduce these to natural gifts is to rob the church of the power tools of the spirit necessary to edify people and build God's Kingdom. What God has called us to do absolutely requires dependence upon the working of the Spirit and the display of His power.

A spiritual gift (Greek *charisma*) is given to Christians by God. These *charisma* are gifts of God's grace (*charis*). They are not earned through merit. These are contrasted with fruit, since gifts are given but fruit must be grown. This is why there may be people who have powerful gifts but major character problems. We must never mistake God's working through our gifts as God's approval of every other area of our conduct. This was the problem of the Corinthian church. Nonetheless, we must have spiritual gifts to be fully "established" (Rom. 1:11 KJV) as a complete New Testament Church. Normal Christianity is incomplete without either the gifts or character.

Christians, as members of the Body of Christ, have different gifts (Rom. 12:6) or can be said to operate more regularly with particular gifts. The diversity of gifts among Christians is purposed by God so that members of the church need one another. No Christian or local Church is meant to stand alone apart from the Body of Christ as a whole. God places in others what we ourselves need. We likewise have a responsibility to use the gifts God has entrusted us with (Rom 12:6) to serve others. By each member of the Body giving and receiving in this way, the whole Church grows (Eph. 4:16) and every need can be met.

## The Nine Gifts of the Spirit

In 1 Corinthians 12:8-10, Paul lists nine different gifts of the Holy Spirit. Paul's purpose in writing this chapter is not to give a detailed explanation of the gifts but rather to describe their proper order in the church. Evidently, the Corinthian church was already very familiar with these gifts and what they were. The nine gifts can be divided into three major groups: revelation, power, and utterance.

**Revelation**: Word of Knowledge, Word of Wisdom, Discerning of Spirits

**Power**: Working of Miracles, Gifts of Healings, Faith

**Utterance**: Diverse Tongues, Interpretation of Tongues, Prophecy

The **revelation gifts** specifically concern those gifts that have special insight revealed by the Holy Spirit to a person that they would not naturally perceive or know themselves. A Word of Knowledge is simply a word of God's knowledge about a person or situation. It is not all that God knows, of course, but a piece of information given through the supernatural revelation of the Spirit. The Word of Wisdom is similar in that it is a word of God's revealed wisdom about a person or situation. These two gifts differ in that knowledge deals with the "what" (information) and wisdom deals with the "how" (application or understanding). Discerning of Spirits is special insight into the activity of the spiritual world. When someone exercises this gift, they can recognize whether an activity is the work of the Spirit of God, a demonic spirit, an angel, or a human being (see for example Acts 16:16-18). This is vital to discerning godly supernatural activity from supernatural counterfeits that are originated by something other than God. This gift should not be confused with general discernment which all Christians must develop through experience and maturity (Heb. 5:14).

The **power gifts** are those that involve supernatural action or intervention by God. The working of miracles is the operation of special miracles as was seen in the ministry of Paul (Acts 19:11). It is interesting to note that miracles were becoming so common place in the early church that there was, as in Acts 19, a category called unusual miracles! The gift of faith is not the general faith that all Christians possess, which is something that grows and develops. The gift of faith is a special infusion of faith for a particular moment. This often operates alongside the working of miracles. Lastly, the gifts of healings describe manifestations of the Holy Spirit that result in physical healing. This complements the ministry of believers in laying hands on the sick (Mark 16:18).

The **utterance gifts** are vocal manifestations of the Spirit. The gift of tongues, distinct from a Christian's personal prayer language (see chapter six), is the corporate exercise of a message given in a language not previously learned by speaker. It is to be accompanied by its counterpart gift, the interpretation of tongues, which is the God-given interpretation of a message in tongues. The gift of prophecy is simply the speaking forth of a God given message or word. This is inspired by God's Spirit but is subject to human fallibility and therefore must be tested (1 Thess. 5:21, 1 John 4:1). The gift of prophecy is not authoritative in the sense that Scripture is. However, prophecy is for "upbuilding and encouragement and consolation" (1 Cor. 14:3).

## Receiving Spiritual Gifts

Now that we have looked briefly at what spiritual gifts are, how do we receive them?

Here are six keys to receiving and sustaining the gifts of the Holy Spirit.

## 1. Gifts are given according to will of the Holy Spirit

The Holy Spirit gives gifts "to each one individually as He wills" (1 Cor. 12:11). This illustrates our need for one another's gift and that our gifts ultimately come from God.

## 2. Gifts are often received at the Baptism with the Holy Spirit

For many Christians, the Baptism with the Spirit becomes the entry point to the supernatural power of God. As we examined in chapter five, tongues and prophecy often accompanied the Baptism with the Spirit in Scripture. We should expect the same today. I have known many who, after being baptized with the Spirit, began to experience gifts such as the word of knowledge for the first time. While it is true that we have individual gifts, it is also true that to have the fullness of the Spirit is to have access to all the gifts when needed. More on this in the next point.

## 3. We must earnestly desire the gifts

*Pursue love, and earnestly desire the spiritual gifts, especially that you may prophesy.*

1 Corinthians 14:1

We must pursue love (the fruit of the Spirit, character) and desire spiritual gifts. We are to have a strong desire to experience and be used of God in these areas. The fact that we are to desire particular gifts like prophecy implies that, even though God sovereignly distributes gifts to individuals for regularly use, we may legitimately pursue particular gifts as needed. All the gifts are available to us as needed for the edification of others, while certain members function in specific gifts more regularly. Never assume because you have not yet experienced a gift that God has sovereignly determined not to give that to you.

1 Cor. 12:31 likewise instructs us to desire the best gifts. How can it be said that some gifts are the best? No gift is necessarily better than another in quality but may be better in that it is more appropriate for meeting a particular need. We should not want some gifts because others seem inferior but should desire whatever gifts that are best suited to the need before us. For example, when I am visiting a sick person in the hospital, the best gift would be a gift of healing. For corporate worship, as in Paul's letter, the best gift would be prophecy rather than tongues without interpretation because people need to understand the word from God to be edified. Because you have the Holy Spirit, you can desire and believe God for the right gift for the right situation as well as grow in the gifts that God has given you for more regular exercise among the Body.

## 4. Gifts are received through impartation

*For I long to see you, that I may impart unto you some spiritual gift, to the end ye may be established*

Romans 1:11 KJV

One of the clearest Scriptural methods of receiving spiritual gifts is through impartation. Impartation deals more with what is "caught" than what is "taught". Paul the Apostle desired to be present with the church at Rome to impart a spiritual gift. When he wrote to Timothy, his spiritual son, Paul made reference twice to spiritual gifts and impartation. He reminded Timothy of "the gift of God which is in you through the laying on of my hands" (2 Tim. 1:6) and "which was given you by prophecy when the council of elders laid their hands on you" (1 Tim. 4:14). Both of these were likely references to the same impartation during the commissioning of Timothy to his ministry. Timothy received a spiritual gift through the laying on of hands.

## 5. Gifts operate in an atmosphere of faith

We can both receive and sustain the manifestation of the Spirit only in an atmosphere of faith. Faith is our confident expectation of what God can and will do in our midst. Environments where there is little faith for the operation of the gifts of the Spirit will have little or no manifestation of them. We will "prophesy according to the proportion of faith" that we possess (Rom. 12:6). We can experience as much of God's Spirit as we believe Him for. Likewise, Jesus often stated that what people experienced supernaturally was according to their faith (Matt. 9:29).

## 6. You must stir up or exercise existing, dormant gifts

An important key to sustaining our spiritual gifts is to simply keep using them. Like a muscle that atrophies through inactivity, spiritual gifts become dormant when they are neglected. Timothy evidently did this and so was instructed by Paul to "stir up the gift of God" (2 Tim. 1:6 KJV). Many Christians, because of fear or neglect have buried their "talent" and laid aside their spiritual gifts. We must remember that we are to minister, that is serve, each other with our gifts "as good stewards of the manifold grace of God." (1 Pet. 4:10 KJV) As stewards, our gifts belong to Him; and we are ultimately accountable to God to use and not neglect them.

## Growing in the Gifts

For Christians to become mature in the expression of spiritual gifts, we must regularly exercise them in an environment of honor, love, accountability, and safety. While giving everyone in the church practice is not always possible in a larger church service, there can and should be opportunities in smaller groups and classes where Christians can learn and practice their gifts to edify one another and build their faith to be used by God in the church and world.

Many have a bad taste in their mouth concerning spiritual gifts because of misuse and abuse. However, we must take Paul's admonition to heart:

*Do not quench the Spirit. Do not despise prophecies, but test everything; hold fast what is good.*

1 Thessalonians 5:19-21

## Chapter 9

# The River of the Spirit

In Ezekiel 47, the prophet Ezekiel is shown a tremendous vision of a great river flowing east from the Temple in Jerusalem. This water flows out from the House of God to the Great Sea; and the further it flows from the Temple, deeper the river becomes. This river is a powerful picture of the Person and ministry of the Holy Spirit flowing from His Temple, the Church. We are the House of God individually and corporately (1 Cor. 3:16, 1 Pet. 2:4-6, 1 Tim. 3:15). From the sanctuary in our hearts, where His presence dwells, God's river pours out to a world that so desperately needs Him.

We must have the fullness of God's Spirit in our lives, not only for us but for the world around us that God longs to touch. Jesus declared that "Whoever believes in me, as the

Scripture has said, out of his heart will

flow rivers of living water" (John 7:38). He was referring to the

Holy Spirit (John 7:39) that was to flow out of our hearts like a

river. Your life is a move of God waiting to happen.

I long for the day when Christianity will go beyond

mere intellectual assent to the doctrine of the Spirit and fully

experience the implications of the world changing truth that

God Himself dwells in us. What if we really knew and

understood that the God Who created the universe stepped

into the grocery store with us the moment we entered the

building?

Rivers have the power to transform entire

environments. Likewise the Spirit of God within us has the

power to change individuals, families, and nations wherever He

goes. The only question is, will we open the door of our hearts

and let Him flow out of us? Many of us are waiting for God to

change the world. God is waiting for us to release His river. As

Ezekiel's vision illustrates, where the river flows there is healing

for the nations and a great harvest of souls (Ezek. 47:7-10).

What the church could not do over 2,000 years with all of our best methods and traditions, God's Spirit can do in a moment of outpouring.

Where the river stops flowing, however, that area becomes a marsh (Ezek. 47:11). This illustrates what happens when we as Christians individually and corporately stop releasing the river and refuse to freely giving what we have received. Church history is littered with the relics of movements that became monuments simply because men stopped being led by God and letting Him flow through them in a new way.

As we conclude this study, we must notice an important invitation that is implied in Ezekiel's prophecy. As the river is measured from the threshold of the Temple, Ezekiel finds that the water gets deeper every thousand cubits. The further along the river he goes, the deeper things get until at last he has to swim and cannot wade through the water remaining on his own feet. There is more to the Holy Spirit than the church has ever known. We must go deeper in the things of God. We must be willing to surrender complete control to God and let Him carry us in the current of His Spirit. This will mean less dependence on our abilities and far more dependence on the Spirit. The adventure of this Spirit-filled life beckons.

Are you ready to go deeper?

## About the Author

**Brian Rezendes** is a pastor, Bible teacher, and founder of The Ekklesia Toolbox. He is married to Jenna Rezendes. They have three children Samuel, William, and Elizabeth.

Made in the USA
Middletown, DE
07 September 2022

72453803R00054